DETROIT
PUBLIC
LIBRARY

APR   1996

CH

DETROIT

VISIONS OF THE EAGLE

*As an eagle views the world
from its lofty perch,
soaring and swooping to capture prey,
so does Dale Fisher examine
a subject from his own domain,
capturing its beauty and detail
with a keenness of vision
matching that of the majestic bird.*

The Photographic Art of
DALE FISHER

Creative Flying by Brian McMahon and Pat Mullen
Text and Creative Direction by Mary Beth Fisher

Text & Creative Direction: Mary Beth Fisher
Graphic Designer: Pat Truzzi

Printed in Michigan, USA
by ImageMasters Precision Printing

ISBN 0-9615623-3-1
Library of Congress Catalog Card Number 94-61438

All images in this book are available as framed photographic art
in sizes from 16"x20" to 38"x48" or in murals up to eight
feet long. An extensive collection of other Open and Limited
Edition photographic art from Arizona, Florida, Hawaii,
Michigan and New York is also available. Contact Dale Fisher
Gallery for current prices and additional information.

Address all inquiries to:
Eyry of the Eagle Publishing
Dale Fisher Gallery
1916 Norvell Road
Grass Lake, MI 49240

(517) 522-3705
FAX: (517) 522-4665

Other books by Dale Fisher:

Detroit (Published in 1985; now out of print)
Hard cover, 178 pages, 139 color photographs

Michigan: From the Eyry of the Eagle
Hard cover, 146 pages, 119 color photographs – $60

Mackinac Island
Soft cover, portfolio of 16 frameable 9 x 12 prints. – $15

LIBERTY; Visions of the Eagle
Soft cover, 40 pages, 21 color photographs – $12

Books in progress:

NEW YORK: Visions of the Eagle
ANN ARBOR: Visions of the Eagle
HAWAII: Visions of the Eagle

Production Information

Color Separations, Total Prepress and Print
Production by ImageMasters Precision Printing
using:

Crosfield Magnascan Plus
High Resolution Color Scanner

Crosfield MagnaSetter 750 Image Setter
at 300 lines per inch

DuPont Waterproof Proofing System
on Actual Stock

Mitsubishi 3F 40" Waterless 6-color Press

Negative Waterless Plates by Toray

Kohl-Madden Waterless Ink and Archival
Spot Varnish

Stock from Seaman-Patrick Paper Company
Gleneagle 80# Gloss Text
Consort Royal Brilliance 100# Text Dust Jacket

Binding by Rand McNally

To Mary Beth
whose book this really is
and to
Debra Sue
Kimberle Ann
and
Matthew Dale

Foreword

When I was a young girl, I was hired by a downtown Detroit building management firm. To my surprise I found I could see the Detroit River from the office windows. What a view! I was excited to work in the heart of our city because I realized it was the pulse beat of the community, the center of all the retail, banking, government and business activity. And just on the other side of the river was that great neighbor of ours, Canada. It took only two minutes to travel through the tunnel into another country.

Occasionally, when I would gaze out along the riverfront and saw all the surface parking lots, warehouses and dilapidated buildings, I would be sad. I thought it was a tremendous waste to use the land along this beautiful river in this way. I wondered, "will it ever change?" As the years went by, it did change, little by little. Many of the visionary leaders in our city during the past five decades slowly and deliberately, but consistently, changed the face of the riverfront. The parking lots disappeared. The obsolete warehouses, buildings and eyesores were removed. In their place emerged Historic Mariners' Church, Cobo Center, Ford Auditorium, Veterans Memorial Building, the Renaissance Center, Joe Louis Arena, the Riverfront Apartments, Harbortown Village, Chene Park, St. Aubin Park, Stroh's River Place, et cetera. Pedestrians and visitors now have a pleasant walkway along the river. Detroiters now have a riverfront of which they can be proud. And adding to our delight is the necklace of twinkling lights on the Ambassador Bridge, symbolizing the friendship between Canada and the United States.

So, when Dale and Mary Beth Fisher invited me to write the foreword to this wonderful book which they have created, my mind's eye traveled back over the years to recall what the riverfront once was, and how it has changed to become what it is today. Granted, we still have some obsolete buildings and too many surface parking lots, but we do have a far more attractive riverfront that has spilled over into the heart of the city. And its potential is yet to be reached. As I looked at the breathtaking photographs taken by Dale from a helicopter, which reflect the beauty of the past and the present, I thought about the new spirit that is so evident in our City. I reflected that we can never arrive at the present unless we journey through the past. And time and nature have presented us at this period of our history with a great deal of beauty.

Just as the leaders of the past, one by one, were able to make their visions a reality by constructing new buildings and monuments, I know so will the leaders of today and tomorrow. The efforts of the past assure us that a constant effort to create a better community, which represents the best of the old and the new, will continue. Inherently, time has played its role in these changes, and through these photographs I sense a deeper commitment to our future. For when you take the ingredients of joy, beauty and hope and mix them all together, seemingly with something as mundane as economic development, the obsolete disappears and the future emerges for the better.

Books are priceless. So, to Dale and Mary Beth Fisher, thank you for providing our community with this treasure which expresses the past, the present and what we can look forward to in the future.

Diane J. Edgecomb
President, Central Business District Association

4

Introduction

A spirit of energy and optimism has swept over the city of Detroit and the surrounding metropolitan area, so real you can almost reach out and touch it. It is obvious in the many development and redevelopment projects, the residential building boom, the attraction of new business, and the national and international events that have occurred here. It is in this exciting atmosphere of revitalization that we made the decision to produce a brand new book on Detroit to replace our earlier 1985 version, now out of print.

The unique perspective of these photographs, all taken from a helicopter, depicts the natural and man-made beauty of the metropolitan area in a way that is fresh and new even to the critical viewer. Many of the scenes will be recognizable, others may be totally new, and even the familiar will show geographic relationships perhaps not seen before. As expressed in the subtitle, the tour we are about to give you is analogous to the view of a majestic eagle as it soars, swoops and circles over Detroit and the surrounding area.

Because of the nature of this photography and the space limitations of a single volume, we endeavor only to give an overall impression of what is available in this great city. The Detroit metropolitan area has more wonderful attractions, beautiful neighborhoods and impressive commercial projects than we can possibly show on these pages, and there are many, many more wonderful photographs for which we unfortunately had no room.

Along with factual captions, we have added personal commentary from those who know the subject best—Detroiters who love their city and its treasures. Some names you may recognize, others you may not, but all authors describe a city of strength, beauty, innovation and caring people.

In the nearly 300 years since its founding, Detroit has grown from a tiny settlement of fur traders to an industrial giant in a global economy. It has prospered because of its countless visionary leaders and generations of creative and hard-working citizens. As we approach our tercentenary in July, 2001, Detroit is once again on the move, marshalling its talent and resources to assure its continued position as a world-class city in the 21st century.

Dale and Mary Beth Fisher

Acknowledgments

This project has involved the support, advice, expertise and hard work of many, many people to whom we owe our heartfelt thanks. Without their assistance, it would not have become a reality.

First and foremost, to Diane Edgecomb for her enthusiasm, sage advice, continuous support and countless hours of labor on many phases of the book. To her wonderful CBDA staff who graciously and generously assisted us in a variety of ways. To the Central Business District Association and Greater Detroit Chamber of Commerce member companies and other Corporate Sponsors *(see list opposite)* whose commitment to this book enabled it to be printed. To Phil Boyce, Joel Alexander, J.P. McCarthy, "Fat Bob" Taylor and all at WJR Radio who promoted the book and assisted us in obtaining wonderful quotations from metropolitan Detroiters. To those terrific authors who sent us inspiring thoughts on Detroit, including those that were used and those for which, unfortunately, there was not adequate space. To Jill DeMaris of Detroit Upbeat who worked tenaciously on our behalf and whose love of, and knowledge about, the city added immeasurably to the text. To Detroiters at Heart members Bob Jackman, Marguerite Hague, Karen Menard and Andrea Petlichkoff who contributed caption information. To Spike Bell for his wonderful photograph of Detroit from Windsor during the International Freedom Festival *(pages 130-31)*. To Bryan Smith for his photographs of Dale, Brian and Pat *(pages 8-9 and dust jacket)*. To Tim Donovan, salesman *extraordinaire,* for his expert assistance. To Ellen Shook and Seaman-Patrick Paper Company for their generous assistance and support. To those who lent their expertise and assisted us in a number of different ways: Melvin Hollowell, Jeff Johns, Rebecca Kennerly, Christine Mack, Linda Mahoney, the Matthew Peak family, Jim Rooke, Cory Sarrault, Vicki Spannagel, Cary Wolfinger, and others too numerous to mention.

Special thanks go to those talented and hard-working individuals and organizations who faithfully translated the artist's images and brought this work to print. To our designer, Pat Truzzi, for accomplishing her monumental task beautifully, on time and with unending patience and good humor. To her husband, Marcello, for his assistance and understanding throughout the long hours. To our photographic color printer, Chuck Edwards, whose darkroom artistry produced superb reproduction prints, and to Mike Wolf and the Precision Photographics staff who committed to our tight deadlines. To Ken Guldi, whose talent and diligence produced exceptional color separations from reflective art (an especially difficult challenge); to Julie Leonhard, Kevin Krueger, Anatole Ostrovsky, Dave Sheets, Tom and Gary Bomek, Mike Lahti, Tim Price, Bob Riordan, Greg Dupke, Vladimir Gazizov and the entire ImageMasters Precision Printing staff who invested themselves personally in making this book the best that it could be, while extending gracious hospitality throughout the printing process. And finally, to Jeanne Stiles, Mary Manning and the Rand McNally staff for their valuable assistance and beautiful binding.

Corporate Sponsors

AAA Michigan
Albert Kahn Associates
Ambassador Bridge
American Natural Resources
Ameritech
Arthur Andersen & Company
Becker Group, Inc.
Central Business District Association
Chrysler Corporation
Comerica Bank
Detroit & Canada Tunnel Corporation
Detroit Free Press
Detroit Marine Terminals, Inc.
Detroit Medical Center
Detroit/Wayne County Port Authority
Du Pont Printing & Publishing
Electronic Data Systems
Ford Motor Company
Freudenberg-NOK
Friedman Companies
General Motors Corporation
Ghafari Associates, Inc.
Greater Detroit Chamber of Commerce
Greenfield Die and Manufacturing Corp.
Henry Ford Health System
Hubble, Roth & Clark, Inc.
ImageMasters Precision Printing
Johnson Controls, Inc.
LovioGeorge Inc.
Marquette Building Redevelopment
McDonald's Corporation
MPI International, Inc.
NBD Bank
Northwest Airlines
Precision Photographics
Ring Screw Works
Rivertown Business Association
Rockwell International
Seaman-Patrick Paper Company
St. John's Episcopal Church
Stroh Brewery
SymCon
Talon Group
The Renaissance Club
The Taubman Company
Total Petroleum, Inc.
Total Travel Management, Inc.
United Technologies Automotive, Inc.
William Burke
WJR Radio

The Photographer

Dale Fisher sees the world as few others do—he is perhaps the only artist photographer in the world who works exclusively from a helicopter. Born in Ann Arbor and trained in aerial reconnaissance photography by the Navy, he has been perfecting his art since 1954.

Combining artistic vision with his perspective from above, Dale transforms such mundane subjects as freeways, rooftops and parked vehicles into colorful graphic patterns. He works with color, light and shadow to create magnificent images out of freighters on the river or horses grazing in a pasture—and all the while, skimming over his subject at ground speeds up to 120 miles per hour! Shunning special filters and photographic gimmicks, Dale uses a normal lens and slow speed film for most of his work, with a telephoto lens or panoramic camera reserved for special situations. His shutter speeds can be as slow as a fifteenth of a second for early morning or late evening scenes.

Dale resides with his wife, Mary Beth, on the *Eyry of the Eagle Farm* in Grass Lake, Michigan, where a collection of his open and limited edition photographic art hangs in the Dale Fisher Gallery, a restored 100-year-old barn. His work also hangs in the collections of many U.S. corporations, institutions and individuals. Previous books include *Detroit* and *MICHIGAN: From the Eyry of the Eagle.* In addition to this book, Dale has recently completed *LIBERTY: Visions of the Eagle,* a photographic essay on the Statue, and is currently working on books on New York, Ann Arbor and Hawaii.

The Pilots

Brian McMahon, owner of McMahon Helicopter Services, is, in Dale's estimation, the finest photographic helicopter pilot in the world. Working together for more than eighteen years, Brian and Dale have mastered the intense concentration, coordination and other skills required for creating photographic art from a helicopter.

Pat Mullen, chief pilot at McMahon Helicopter Services, began his flying career as a combat helicopter pilot in Vietnam, serving in the same unit with Brian McMahon. He switched from an earlier career in health care to pursue his passion for flying and has developed great skill as a photographic pilot.

The Producers

Mary Beth Fisher *(right)*, Executive Director of Dale Fisher Gallery, combines writing and editing abilities with her background in photography and marketing communications to author text and direct all creative and production aspects of Dale's published work. Born and raised in Detroit and a direct descendant of one of its founding settlers, this book is, for her, a labor of love.

Pat Truzzi *(left)*, an award-winning graphic designer, illustrator and watercolor artist, has created elegant design solutions to complex communications problems for more than twenty-five years. Her uncommon level of experience and expertise has contributed to the success of numerous businesses and organizations, both locally and nationally.

"Along with Detroit's long history as a progressive city, an industrial city, a city of culture, good will and good people, is the fact that Detroit is a beautiful city. We have long been a great place in which to live, work, do business, raise our children and prosper. Detroit has witnessed many great days and our best days lie ahead."

Dennis W. Archer
Mayor
City of Detroit

On July 24, 1701, explorer Antoine de la Mothe Cadillac canoed with 100 soldiers and fur traders from Montreal to establish a fur trading center they called Fort-Pontchartrain-du-d'etroit. During the almost 300 years since its founding, Detroit has grown and prospered, weathering some difficult times along the way. Once again, the city is engaged in an important period of revitalization, buoyed by the energy, optimism, and enthusiasm of its strong and resourceful citizens.

"One cold, snowy February afternoon, as two pregnant friends and I were driving home from the Fisher Theatre, my car developed a flat tire on the expressway. We waited and eventually two young men appeared on the overpass above us and came down and changed the tire for us. I tried to pay them for their help, but they wouldn't accept any money. 'Instead,' they said, 'just say something nice about Detroit.' When I heard about this book, I decided this was my perfect opportunity!"

Barbara Manko
Bloomfield Hills, MI

(Overleaf)
"Since people from all over the world visit The Poster Gallery while in the Fisher Building, I get to experience their delight—sometimes even surprise—about the wonderful things in Detroit of which they were previously unaware: great architecture, fine restaurants, unique shopping and friendly people."

Edith Kaufman
Owner, The Poster Gallery, Detroit

As one might expect, the Motor City has designed an extensive and very efficient roadway system to transport both its citizens and its products. From east to west, north to south, connecting expressways, such as the John C. Lodge and I-94 *(opposite)*, expedite commuters and trucks to their destinations in the city and its suburbs. I-696 *(above)* includes several wide overpasses with beautifully landscaped parks to facilitate pedestrian access across the expressway and enhance the area for its residents.

Overleaf: Dawn breaks on the Fisher Building, General Motors World Headquarters and other New Center area businesses and homes while downtown skyscrapers await the bustle of the business day.

"Detroit has many hidden qualities—one of which is its people. I am impressed
by how readily the Detroit community welcomes a newcomer into its activities."

Jerome P. Montopoli
Managing Partner, Arthur Andersen & Company
(Moved to Detroit from Cincinnati, Ohio, in March 1992)

"Detroit has the strength of a lion and the elegance of a swan."

Charles E. Harvey
Clinton Township, MI

Developed by Gerald Hines of Dallas and completed in 1992, One
Detroit Center at Larned and Woodward is the newest skyscraper on
Detroit's skyline. The three courageous workman *(above)* and the *Spirit
of Detroit* sculpture in the lower right *(opposite)*, clearly indicate the
building's imposing size. Major tenants include Comerica Bank, Arthur
Andersen & Company and J. Walter Thompson Advertising Agency.

Overleaf: The rising sun highlights the varied architecture of Detroit's
downtown buildings with its warm glow. Windsor, our Canadian
neighbor, lies just across the river.

"In 1927 I began going to the Eastern Market to sell produce from our farm with my parents. At that time, horse-drawn wagons and push carts were used. Now farmers come hundreds of miles to sell their products. On Saturdays people by the thousands come to do their shopping. Many ethnic stores surround the Market, and it is still one of the historic places of Detroit."

Lawrence Zienert
Washington, MI

"I've been shopping at the Eastern Market for more than fifty years. It's one of my favorite places in Detroit. The meat and produce can't be beat and you meet people from all over the city and of almost every ethnic background you can imagine. And the Flower Days in May are a sight to behold!"

Betty Donovan
Detroit

For more than a century, generations of farmers from all over Michigan and Ontario have brought their fresh goods to Detroit's citizenry at the Eastern Market. A wide array of specialty stores also offer hard-to-find imported foods and locally-made smoked meats and cheeses in a charming and friendly atmosphere.

Located on the edge of the Eastern Market, Historic Trinity Lutheran Church *(above)* was founded by the German residents of Detroit's first ethnic neighborhood. Today it is still a thriving parish, with parishioners from the city and suburbs alike, and it features an outstanding Christmas display during the holiday season. The adjacent Grand Trunk Railroad Building wraps its modern structure protectively around the beautiful church.

Close by on Gratiot Avenue, Brewery Park *(opposite)* is bathed in early morning light. This office complex was developed in the 1980s by Kirco and Stroh on the site of the old brewery. Tenants include R.L. Polk, United American Health Care and Grand Trunk Railroad.

Overleaf: Off Jefferson, at the foot of Joseph Campau Street, major renovations combine with new construction to create a wonderful commercial and housing district. Talon Center, The Rattlesnake Club Restaurant, Riverplace Hotel and the Detroit Artist's Market are all part of Rivertown, once known as "the warehouse district."

Detroit's neighborhoods are its heart and the rich ethnic heritage of this city is one of its major strengths. Corktown, Greektown, Bricktown and Hamtramck are some of the older enclaves that still retain their strong ethnic tradition. Many more exist within the city and surrounding suburbs.

Neighborhoods nurture their children who are the future of all cities. Victoria Park, a brand new subdivision on Detroit's east side *(above)* and the older established one surrounding Central High School and Durfee Middle School *(opposite)* are but two examples of strong communities in this city.

Overleaf: This inspiring sculpture by G. Goodacre sits proudly in front of Talon Center in Rivertown. Several other wonderful pieces of art, both outside and inside the building complex, enrich this urban area.

"I have always been captivated by this particular sculpture *(overleaf)* because it inspires so many profound images and thoughts.

First, you are struck by the innocence, diversity and intensity of the children as they gaze upward at our nation's flag. This piece reminds us that our children are our future; and it is the hopes and dreams you see in their eyes that will shape that future. It is also a solemn reminder of the enormous sacrifices so many have made so that we can cherish and enjoy the freedoms and the free enterprise system we have today.

It seems appropriate that this wonderful work of art found its home on Detroit's historic riverfront, for just as this sculpture inspires thoughts of hope, vision and unity, it also reminds us that it is these same enduring qualities that will deliver the promise and potential of our great city."

Randolph J. Agley, Chairman, Talon Inc., Detroit

"Lafayette Park is unquestionably one of the most vibrant neighborhoods in Detroit. World-renowned architect Ludwig Mies Van derRohe planned the area, and it functions as a totally integrated community where people from a range of socioeconomic, racial and age groups live in harmony. There is an abundance of amenities including schools, churches and shops. Also, destinations such as Rivertown, the Eastern Market and Greektown are all within a ten minute walk. Perhaps the best thing about the area is Lafayette Park itself which is active year-round from sunrise well into sunset with walkers, joggers, sunbathers, children playing, picnics, softball, volleyball, basketball and tennis. It's a great place to live, especially if you work downtown, and property values have remained very stable over the years."

Alan Scott White
Lafayette Towers
Detroit

Historic Indian Village *(opposite)* was once the residence of many auto magnates. Pewabic tiles from Detroit's own unique pottery and beautiful craftsmanship decorate many of the homes in this still popular and thriving community.

Both Indian Village and the Lafayette Park area *(above)* provide a wide variety of housing: from stately older homes to modern apartments, townhouses and condominiums. Their proximity to the Detroit River and downtown Detroit attractions make them a desirable location for professionals, families and retirees alike.

DETROIT

31

"Through these Detroit straits, where French Canadian voyageurs passed warily through wild Indian country with fur-laden canoes, now flows a steady stream of maritime and lake freighters carrying their cargoes to all ports of the five Great Lakes.

Up river to the East, beyond the tall rise of Renaissance Center towers, once flourished world-class manufactories of stoves, varnishes, seeds and pharmaceuticals… given over now to park sites, restaurants, apartments and far-sighted developmental planning. Further along, bordering on Lake St. Clair, lies beautiful Belle Isle park, annual host to the cars of the Grand Prix circuit, Gold Cup hydroplanes, and countless hordes of picnic goers."

Henry L. Despard
Birmingham, MI

Dotting the largest city-owned island park in the country *(opposite)* are many beautiful trees planted over the years by the Friends of Belle Isle. Many of these trees were donated as living memorials to loved ones by metro Detroit residents. The Japanese Society of Detroit also recently donated one hundred cherry trees which have been planted near Belle Isle's Scott Fountain. The Detroit Yacht Club *(above)*, largest inland yacht club in the country (360 boat slips) and the Detroit Boat Club, the nation's oldest, are also located on Belle Isle.

Overleaf: **Between East Jefferson Avenue and the river, opposite Belle Isle, is Harbortown, a lovely self-contained residential community of apartments, condominiums, shops and services. Watching maritime traffic is a favorite pastime of many Harbortown residents.**

"I like boating, especially on sail boats, on the fresh waters of nearby Lake St. Clair and the Detroit River. Unknown to most residents, there is a scheduled sail boat race on the Lake nearly every day of the week, June through September. It's great recreation! I can leave my office downtown at normal shut-down time and enjoy an evening race or cruise an hour later. The abundance of fresh water with navigational connections to other Great Lakes makes me excited about Detroit!"

Curt Lundy
Geologist
Detroit

Many apartment buildings, housing developments and marinas line the riverfront and Lake St. Clair, offering area residents boating and water sports "right in their own backyards." Michigan has the largest freshwater fleet in the nation and the annual yacht race to Mackinac Island, hosted by Bay View Yacht Club (*above*), draws participants from the entire Great Lakes Area.

"Spirit of Detroit Thunderfest is composed of over 400 volunteers who are dedicated to improving the image of Detroit by putting on the best civic event in the country. Our organization is totally dedicated to the sport of hydroplane racing and to the city of Detroit, which was its breeding ground."

Jim Garza
Deputy Chairman,
Spirit of Detroit Thunderfest, Inc.

Hydroplanes, *(opposite, right)* **the world's fastest boats, race on the Detroit River each June as part of Spirit of Detroit Thunderfest, a week-long series of events. A huge audience lines the shore and pleasure boats surround the course for the annual Gold Cup race.**

Overleafs: **The hydroplanes' incredible speed is evident in the "roostertail" wakes which almost obliterate them from view. Detroit's landmark on the riverfront drew its name from this phenomenon.**

Stony Creek Metropark in Oakland and Macomb counties *(above)* is one of thirteen Metroparks in a five-county area operated by the Huron-Clinton Metropolitan Authority. Picnicking, swimming, canoeing, nature trails and winter sports are a few of the activities offered.

Many campgrounds are also located within a short drive of almost anywhere in the city. These Boy Scouts *(above)* pitched theirs near Historic Fort Wayne on the Detroit River.

Recently completed St. Aubin Park on the Detroit River *(opposite)* is part of the city's Three-link Park Project. Its focus is fishing and a marina, as opposed to Chene Park which is geared towards entertainment. In keeping with its theme, St. Aubin Park's walkways include imprints of various fish indigenous to the Great Lakes.

Overleaf: Further east along Jefferson Avenue is the Chrysler Jefferson North Assembly plant, one of two auto plants located within the city limits of Detroit. Completed in 1991 on the 283-acre site of the old Jefferson plant, it is the first new plant built by Chrysler in 26 years. Workers there will produce 306,000 Jeep Grand Cherokee sport utility vehicles next year.

Detroit is home to the World Headquarters of three major U.S. auto companies: General Motors Corporation, Ford Motor Company and Chrysler Corporation. Soaring demand, especially for pickup trucks, vans and utility vehicles, has recently caused the "Big Three" to add production shifts. Truck production at Ford's Wayne plant *(opposite),* GM's plant in Pontiac *(right)* and Chrysler's Dodge truck plant in Warren is running at peak capacity to keep up with market demand.

Overleaf: Dawn paints a rosy glow on the Ford Rouge complex. This is the birthplace of Henry Ford's first assembly line, his daring new concept which enabled mass production and lowered the cost to make automobiles affordable to all. This site is also where Ford implemented his philosophy of building an automobile from the raw materials to the finished product. He even went so far as to buy a rubber plantation in South America.

"From my office in Ford's World Headquarters *(overleaf)* I have what has to be the best view of the city there is. I often find myself looking out at Ford's Rouge Complex, and beyond that to the Detroit skyline, and thinking about the early days of the auto industry and the city. Both grew up and rose to world prominence together, and both have been through good times and bad.

The auto industry and Detroit still face many challenges today. But the Ford employees who turn out world-class products from the Rouge and all the other Ford plants in this area every day have shown me what the people of metropolitan Detroit can do when they work together as a team to be the best. I think the future will be bright for Detroit."

Alex Trotman
Chairman and CEO, Ford Motor Company

The Ford Motor Company was founded in Dearborn in 1903 by Henry Ford whose creation of the assembly line process for building automobiles became the model for all types of manufacturing worldwide. Ford's Automotive Components Division is headquartered in Regent Court *(opposite)*, a beautiful new building on its World Headquarters campus.

Early morning light emphasizes the graceful curves and distinctive landscaping of Ghafari and Associates, *(above)*, an architectural and engineering firm located just across Michigan Avenue from Ford World Headquarters.

Overleaf: Sunrise illuminates "The Glass House," Ford Motor Company's World Headquarters. Employer of 322,000 worldwide, Ford produces six million vehicles annually. With plants and other facilities in thirty countries, they sell vehicles in more than 200 markets.

DETROIT

Dearborn, birthplace in 1863 of Henry Ford, is linked inextricably to the company he founded. Fair Lane (*opposite*), a national historic landmark, was the final home of Henry and Clara Ford. The University of Michigan now manages this handsome estate, offering tours of the mansion and making it available for special events.

AAA Michigan (*above*) is headquartered in Dearborn, near Fairlane Town Center, a sprawling shopping mall. Opened nearby in 1989, the Ritz Carlton Dearborn Hotel (*also above*) is elegantly appointed and boasts a fine art collection.

"Detroit has a proud history of idealism, determination, and achievement. In this dynamic environment, pioneers such as Henry Ford were inspired to dream and to create innovations that changed the world forever."

Melvin Hollowell
Attorney and Community Activist
Detroit

The Henry Ford Museum and Greenfield Village, founded in 1929 by Henry Ford, depicts and interprets America's change from a rural, agrarian society to a highly industrialized nation. Its 81-acre outdoor display contains more than 80 historic structures, many of them moved here by Henry Ford. Highlights include several demonstration barns and the Harvey Firestone Farm *(opposite)*, as well as Thomas Edison's Menlo Park laboratory complex, the Wright Brothers Cycle Shop and the Sir John Bennett building *(above)*. Rides around the Lagoon on the Suwanee steamboat *(above)* and other older modes of transportation carry visitors into the past. The Henry Ford Museum contains 12 acres of indoor exhibits on transportation, home arts, furniture, lighting and communications. Together they are the most visited indoor/outdoor historical complex in North America, welcoming more than one million visitors a year.

"We have been making Detroit our principal international gateway. Detroit has become Northwest's largest hub, and we see tremendous potential for this city."

Don Washburn
Executive Vice President-Customer Service
Northwest Airlines

Previous pages: **Just a short distance away in Romulus is Detroit Metropolitan Airport, one of the largest airports in the nation and the major hub of Northwest Airlines. Northwest and its regional airline partners, together with KLM Royal Dutch Airlines, form the world's third-largest airline system serving more than 350 cities in more than 80 countries on six continents. Northwest currently has more than 340 jet departures daily from Detroit.**

Home of Northland, the nation's first suburban shopping center, Southfield has grown into an important center of commerce. Many major companies such as Northwest Airlines, Bozell Worldwide Inc. and Perini Building Company have offices in the Prudential Town Center Complex *(above and opposite)* which connects with The Radisson Plaza Hotel, a major conference center.

"Because of the metropolitan Detroit community's strong support of, and commitment to, amateur and professional sports, we have been able to attract and successfully host various major events such as the U.S. Figure Skating Championships and World Cup Soccer. As a result of these successes, Detroit is again being recognized both nationally and internationally as a desirable venue to host major sporting events."

Tom Constand
President, Detroit Sports Commission

Detroiters love sports activities of all kinds and opportunities abound in the area to participate in both common and somewhat more unusual athletic pursuits. From swimming at the Southfield Civic Center Pool *(above)* and league games at Softball City *(also above)* to Polo matches at Duns Scotus *(opposite)* and croquet at River Place Hotel, there is something available to suit every taste.

Overleaf: Professional sports are also extremely popular in the motor city. Tiger Stadium, one of America's few remaining classic ballparks, is home to Detroit's oldest sports franchise, the Tigers, which became a charter member of baseball's American League in 1901.

"World Cup USA 1994 gave the metropolitan Detroit area not only the opportunity to host this prestigious event but also to show off our attractions, restaurants and hotels to the international market. And the Motor City's image received a boost worldwide as a leader in technology with the historic indoor grass system. It was a fabulous event."

Jim Duggan
Executive Director,
Michigan Host Committee
Detroit World Cup USA 94

World Cup XV brought visitors from all over the world to the Pontiac Silverdome *(opposite)* to watch their home teams compete. A gigantic Swiss flag hung proudly during the opening game between Switzerland and the USA. Michigan State University developed a special shallow-root grass specifically for this international event. This was the first time soccer was played indoors on grass. The grass was later purchased by Detroit Edison and moved to Belle Isle for a new soccer field there.

The Pontiac Silverdome, world's largest domed stadium, is also home to the Detroit Lions football team and hosts other major special events.

"Metropolitan Detroit, like all of Michigan, is paradise for golfers. The combination of old and new, public and private, includes something for everyone."

Tim Donovan
Novi, MI

Michigan is one of the top golfing states in the country in terms of number of courses. Located within the city itself, the Detroit Golf Club *(opposite)*, whose clubhouse *(above, center)* was designed by Albert Kahn, has two beautiful eighteen-hole courses surrounded by stately and prestigious homes. Evergreen Hills in Southfield *(above, top)* and the Bloomfield Country Club *(above, bottom)* are only two of the many suburban courses in the metro area.

Overleaf: The Detroit Red Wings hockey team plays downtown at Joe Louis Arena on the riverfront, also the site for many other sports and entertainment events. The University of Detroit Mercy Titans basketball team plays their home games next door at Cobo Arena which also hosts numerous other programs and activities. Adjacent Cobo Conference/Exhibition Center is the fifth largest convention center in the country with 2.4 million total square feet.

"As a Sports Car Club of America member who has personally observed the internal operation of every one of the Detroit Grand Prix races, I have been proud of the positive impact the event has had on the rest of the world. A Belgian race official told me on his arrival at the airport for his sixth Detroit Grand Prix, 'Bob, I'm really glad to be back in Detroit.' A prominent European race official commented the Detroit race committee did such a good job that he would like to take us with him to all the races on the circuit. Detroit does many things first class, including running car races."

Bob Jackman
President, Detroiters at Heart

Held every June since 1982, the three-day weekend event culminates with the IndyCar race on Sunday. For ten years, the race was held on downtown Detroit streets, but was moved to Belle Isle *(above)* in 1992. The colorful Starting Grid *(opposite)* gives fans the opportunity to view world-famous cars and drivers up close.

Overleafs: Sponsored by Bacardi Rum and Bayview Yacht Club, the 70th sailing of the Mackinac Island Yacht Race in 1994 drew contestants from throughout the Great Lakes region, many of whom return year after year. In fact, after sailing twenty-five races, participants receive the coveted title of "Old Goat."

Sindbad's is a favorite gathering place for Detroit-area boaters. Summer weekends and special events draw throngs of party-goers to the water's edge.

"GM and Detroit have been through a lot together. We've enjoyed some good times; we've struggled through some tough times. Through it all, GM has been proud to be a key part of Detroit's rich history. Today we're both moving with confidence into another new era. It will be a global era. And once again, Detroit will stand for excellence, innovation and success in bringing the benefits and pleasures of personal mobility to people everywhere."

John F. Smith Jr., CEO and President
General Motors Corporation

From an elevated view in General Motors World Headquarters *(opposite)* can be seen GM's Detroit/ Hamtramck Assembly Center *(above)*. Workers there produce all of the Cadillac front-wheel drive cars *(right)* sold throughout the world.

Cadillac is just one of General Motors' seven North American divisions; others are Buick, Oldsmobile, Pontiac, Chevrolet, GMC Truck and Saturn. The largest of Detroit's "Big Three" auto companies, General Motors employs approximately 700,000 workers worldwide. GM sold 7.9 million vehicles worldwide in 1993.

Overleaf: General Motors Founder, William Durant, commissioned architect Albert Kahn to design this national historic landmark, located in Detroit's New Center and completed in 1920. Just across West Grand Boulevard is the ornate Fisher Building, also designed by Albert Kahn and opened in 1928. At night, its illuminated golden tower can be seen for miles around and is one of Detroit's well-known landmarks.

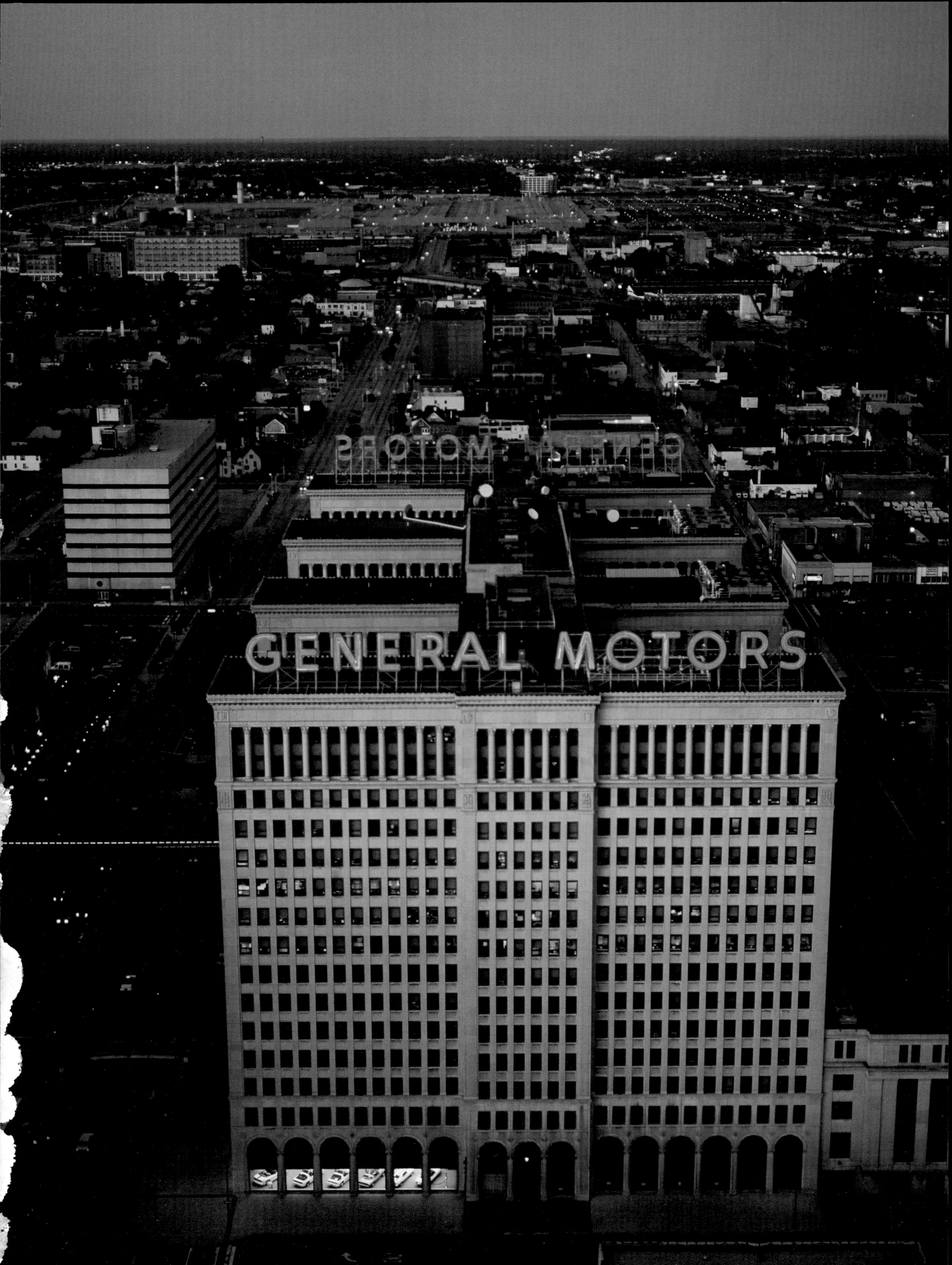
GENERAL MOTORS

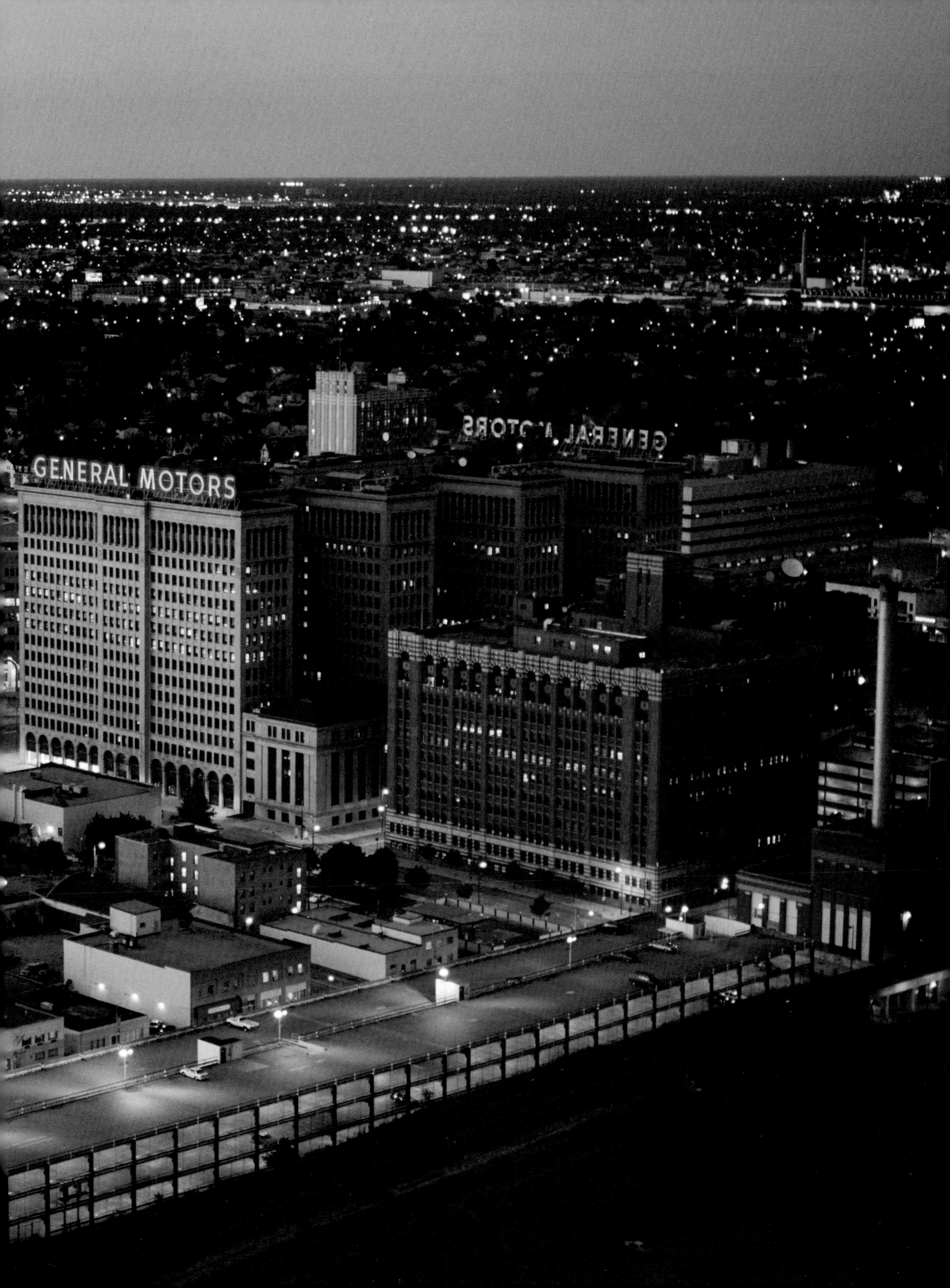
GENERAL MOTORS

General Motors' modern Technical Center *(opposite)* occupies one square mile in Warren and now employs 21,000 people. This research and development facility, which opened its first building in 1950, has grown to include a mile-long test track and a 22-acre lake containing four islands, two fountains and a handsome stainless steel water tower *(right)*. The GM North American Operations Headquarters and its North American Design Center are located there.

"Minutes from downtown and convenient to freeways, New Center
is big business and world-class architecture, top-notch shopping,
dining and entertainment, summer concerts, festive parks and
outdoor cafes. The area is home to the landmark Fisher Building,
General Motors Headquarters, New Center One and Henry Ford
Hospital, as well as the Hotel St. Regis and the Fisher and Attic
Theatres.

Companies have invested over $400 million in reviving the original
1920's vision of a 'New Center' of activity in Detroit. The result is a
great old neighborhood with a great new look: restored homes and
townhouses, seventy shops and restaurants connected by skywalks,
and one of metro Detroit's finest outdoor environments."

Ann Lang
President, New Center Area Council

Michigan TasteFest (*opposite*) **along West Grand Boulevard
in the New Center area is just one of many summer festivals
that Detroiters enjoy. Several of the metro area's best restaurants participate, giving attendees an opportunity to sample
fare from old favorites and newly-discovered establishments
as well. Musical entertainment in front of General Motors
World Headquarters** (*above*) **adds to the festive atmosphere.**

"It's hard to believe, but I've now been waking up the city of Detroit for 30 years. I've seen many changes in Detroit over the years, some good and some not so good. Through it all one thing has never changed: the quality of the citizens of Detroit and Michigan. I feel confident that this city is on the verge of a comeback, and I'm proud and excited to be here to see it happen and take part in it. This is my hometown, and always will be!"

J.P. McCarthy
WJR Radio - AM 760

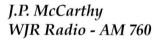

Since 1928, WJR Radio has broadcast from its headquarters in the Fisher Building. The well-known voices of J.P. McCarthy and Fat Bob Taylor *(at JP's annual St. Patrick's Day party above)* and other WJR personalities have become a treasured part of the day for hundreds of thousands of loyal listeners. Tiger baseball broadcasts from "The Voice of the Great Lakes" are beamed throughout Michigan and into neighboring states from their 50,000-watt transmitter.

Overleaf: Just south of the New Center is Wayne State University. Founded in 1868 as Detroit Medical College, it is now Detroit's only research university, offering 4,800 courses in 377 major subject areas. This urban campus is within a few blocks of several other Detroit cultural/educational facilities such as the main branch of the Detroit Public Library, Detroit Institute of Arts, Center for Creative Studies, International Institute, and Detroit Historical Museum, which enrich the education of its students.

"The multifaceted musical life of Detroit reflects the cultural diversity of a city renowned for its contribution to jazz, gospel and pop as well as a variety of ethnic music. In the realm of classical music, Detroit boasts a host of musical organizations including the nationally celebrated Detroit Symphony Orchestra and the Michigan Opera Theatre, scheduled to move into its newly renovated and expanded Detroit Opera House in the spring of 1996. Upon its completion, our city will have the benefits of three world class homes for its cultural institutions: the Detroit Institute of Arts, Orchestra Hall and the Detroit Opera House."

David DiChiera
General Director
Michigan Opera Theatre

"Half a million people visit the Detroit Institute of Arts *(overleaf)* each year, and many of them take the time to fill out comment cards. We take every comment card seriously, because we know that input from our visitors will make visiting the DIA a better experience for everyone. When we were asked for a quote about the DIA, we thought our visitors said it best!"

Samuel Sachs II
Director, DIA

"This is perhaps the greatest collection of art in the world! I am proud to have this place in our city."

"I have come from Europe to Detroit to see the DIA. It is magnificent."

"A wonderful, wonderful place. Congratulations, Detroit!"

For generations many of the world's most outstanding performers have thrilled audiences in the acoustically perfect Masonic Temple Theatre *(above)*. With 4,400 seats and the largest stage in the Midwest, it draws elaborate productions from all over the world to this city.

On a beautiful 315-acre campus in Bloomfield Hills, the Cranbrook Educational Community *(opposite)* is a National Historic Landmark and includes their Academy of Art and Museum, Institute of Science and the Cranbrook House and Gardens. Students from this renowned institution present orchestra, band and vocal concerts, dance and theatrical productions in the Schools' Performing Arts Center.

Overleaf: The Detroit Institute of Arts, one of the five largest art museums in the country, enjoys a worldwide reputation. Diego Rivera's masterpiece mural *Detroit Industry* stands in tribute to the city's workers. A broad range of artistic styles, from classic to modern, are represented in its collection.

"Attending a performance at the Fox is always a thrill for me. I've traveled throughout the United States and all over the world and have never found another theatre that matches its beauty and grandeur."

Dorothy Sweeney
Grosse Pointe, MI

When it was completed in 1861 on what became known as Piety Hill, orchards, farms and a few suburban homes surrounded St. John's Episcopal Church (*above*) on Woodward Avenue. Now this beautiful Victorian Gothic Church lies in the midst of Detroit's theatre district. Its interior is filled with magnificent religious art treasures, including one of the largest and most important examples of mosaic art to be found in this country.

The completely restored Fox Theatre is the catalyst of Detroit's revitalized theatre district (*opposite*). Built in 1928 by William Fox, the 5,000-seat theatre is the second-largest remaining movie palace in the world. With a sumptuous interior modeled on Far Eastern, Egyptian, Babylonian and Indian themes, it offers Broadway, comedy/variety shows, movies and live concerts. Other restored historic venues in the area include Orchestra Hall, home of the Detroit Symphony Orchestra, the Gem Theatre featuring cabaret and live shows, The State Theatre—now a nightclub and entertainment spot, and the landmark Music Hall, offering drama, comedy, dance and children's theater. Michigan Opera Theatre is projected to move in 1996 to the new Michigan Opera House on the site of the old Grand Circus Theatre.

Overleaf: Detroit has been captured on the screen in several movies such as *Beverly Hills Cop* and *Hoffa*. A benefit premiere of Beverly Hills Cop III, attended by celebrities from Hollywood and Detroit, was held here at the Fox.

"Detroit has had a wonderful love affair with its Zoological Park from the beginning. This innovative pioneering facility has provided a magical experience for millions of children and adults and represents a true jewel of the community. This is where we reconnect people and nature and, in so doing, both enhance our lives and ensure wildlife's future."

Ron Kagan
Director, Detroit Zoo

The Detroit Zoological Park *(opposite)* opened in Royal Oak in 1928. It was one of the first zoos to show most of its animals in natural outdoor enclosures without bars and reputed to be one of the finest zoos in the country. Today it houses more than 1,200 animals of more than 300 different species—and continues to add to its exhibits regularly. For example, the polar bears *(above)* are getting an underwater feeding facility where visitors will be able to view them through glass, catching live fish just as they do in their natural habitat. A passenger train *(also above)* facilitates getting around the 125-acre park.

Overleaf: Chene Park Music Theatre at the foot of Chene on the Detroit River, offers top performers and a spectacular view. Concert-goers can sit on the lawn or in the amphitheater and listen to jazz, blues, popular and classical music while watching river traffic pass in the setting sun.

"My mid-century memories of Detroit's special oasis, Belle Isle, are preceded by family involvement in the early 1900's and are followed by my enjoyment of it today. A bike ride from my home, across the bridge, around the luminous white Scott Fountain, and past the casino is a favored way to end the week. Hats off to the original Island planners and builders…applause to those who preserve and maintain it for use by us now."

Linda Leddick, PhD
Detroit Public Schools

Across MacArthur Bridge off Jefferson Avenue is Belle Isle, Detroit's own 980-acre island park. It was purchased by the city in 1879 and designed by Frederick Olmstead, also designer of New York's Central Park. Sports activities like fishing, boating and golf, as well as educational family entertainment such as an aquarium (the nation's oldest), conservatory *(opposite)*, Dossin Great Lakes Museum and the Safari Zoo are there, just minutes away from downtown.

Scott Fountain *(above and left)*, designed by Cass Gilbert, was dedicated in 1925 and named for its donor, James Scott. Recently restored, its basin is Pewabic tile made right in Detroit at the famous pottery. During summer evenings a multi-colored light display creates shimmering waterfalls of many hues.

Overleaf: Windsor residents along the Canadian shoreline opposite Belle Isle have a beautiful view of 'Ville d'etroit' — 'City of the Strait' — as it was called by French explorer Antoine de la Mothe Cadillac and the original settlers.

"For more than six decades, Detroit City Airport has provided quality service. This has been done as a matter of tradition. The airport now has direct service to Cleveland, Akron/Canton, Indianapolis and Chicago. Presently, major efforts are being put toward expanding the Airport and providing more airline service.

As the city moves into the 21st century, Detroit City Airport will play a major role as an economic and transportation center for the Detroit community."

John Clark III
Director, City of Detroit Airport Department

Detroit City Airport *(opposite)* is on the city's east side, just minutes from downtown.

Overleaf: Further east along Lake St. Clair lie the Grosse Pointes and St. Clair Shores, many of whose residents enjoy boating. The Grosse Pointe Yacht Club is a favorite gathering place for boating enthusiasts and non-boaters alike.

"Detroit has been the most misunderstood major city in the U.S. for a very long time. And what a loss that has been for us all! However, with the change of administration and the much improved economy, we have an excellent opportunity to shine once again.

Detroit's extraordinary geographic location on a major waterway, its close proximity to Canada (with NAFTA in place), skilled labor force and abundance of available land, plus its excellent quality of life all bode well for us. If all of these substantive ingredients are managed and directed properly, Detroit can be *the* city of rebirth in the United States by the year 2000."

Jill A. DeMaris
President, Detroit Upbeat, Inc.

Detroit's location on the River connecting Lakes Erie and St. Clair makes it one of the five largest ports in the country. Many industries have grown along this busy waterway which provides transport to their markets. South of Detroit, the city of Wyandotte is best known for its chemical plants . A residential marina *(above)* shares the beautiful riverfront location with industrial facilities there.

The island community of Grosse Ile *(opposite)* lies south of Wyandotte in the River. Once home to a naval air station, it has several historic buildings, stately older homes and its own airport. Recent years have brought much new development to this popular spot.

Overleaf: Further north along the river, on the southern edge of Detroit, is Zug Island, home of Great Lakes Steel. The vessel *George Stinson* unloads taconite at their facility there.

Dale's artistic vision combines with his perspective from above to create picturesque images out of objects that are mundane when viewed from the ground. For example, he transforms construction cranes and a shipping crane *(above)* and automotive parts containers *(opposite)* into vivid industrial graphic art.

"The focus of life in downtown Detroit is the river: an international border, a busy transportation corridor, a waterway that flows and changes as Detroit does. One who has not viewed downtown Detroit from the river has not glimpsed into the soul of this incredible city. The view from the river reflects more than just Detroit's image. It reflects a quiet elegance enveloping the challenge and promise of this diverse community. To live here is to be woven into the vibrant fabric of the city — a life that is uniquely Detroit."

H. Terry Snowday III
Snowday Consulting, Detroit

"The border between the United States and Canada has the reputation for being the friendliest border in the whole world. In 1981, a small group of people from Detroit and Windsor raised the money to connect the two countries with a necklace of lights on the Ambassador Bridge, a symbol of the exceptionally strong relationship between our two countries."

Fred Somes
Chairman, Motor City Electric Company

The Ambassador Bridge joining Detroit with Windsor, Canada, is the longest suspension bridge linking two countries in the world. Engineered and constructed by McClintic-Marshall and opened to traffic in 1929, this bridge is privately owned.

Overleaf: A freighter passing beneath the Ambassador Bridge is greeted by the rising sun as it heads up the Detroit River towards Lake St. Clair. The mailboat, J.W. Westcott, has just delivered mail and supplies to the ship and is returning to its dock at the foot of 24th Street.

"With the Detroit-Windsor Tunnel and the Ambassador Bridge, Detroit is the busiest passenger car and commercial vehicle border crossing between the United States and Canada."

Donald M. Vuchetich
President, Detroit-Windsor Tunnel

The Detroit-Windsor Tunnel *(right)* under the Detroit River, completed in 1930, is the world's first international underwater vehicular tunnel. It joins two great cities *and* two great countries whose citizens pass freely back and forth, many on a daily basis.

Old Mariners' Church, also known as "The Maritime Sailor's Cathedral" *(opposite, upper left)* has served Great Lakes sailors since 1849. In 1955, this national historic landmark was moved on rollers in a parade from Woodbridge and Woodward to its present location to make way for the Civic Center.

In a unique relationship, each summer for almost forty years Detroit and Windsor have jointly celebrated their respective country's birthdays during the International Freedom Festival, an occasion for week-long celebrations in both cities, highlighted by a gigantic fireworks display on the river. A carnival on Windsor's shore *(above)* is perfectly located for a view of the fireworks.

"It's been said that beauty is in the eye of the beholder, and so it is with me every day. No matter the weather, Detroit always makes a special appearance and I get to watch the show from 500 feet. There's nothing like seeing an early morning sunrise on the Renaissance Center or watching the snow fall soft on the concrete and steel. It's as if someone planted seeds and Detroit grew to be the backdrop for Mother Nature. Looking for a picturesque city? Look no further than the Motor City!"

Dennis H. Neubacher
WJR Radio Traffic Copter

Hart Plaza, *(above and opposite)* **in the center of Detroit's Civic Center, was named for Michigan's U.S. Senator Philip A. Hart. It is the scene of the city's major celebrations and festivals. Almost every weekend between April and September there is some event going on there: from a circus, a series of several ethnic festivals, the International Freedom Festival to the renowned Montreaux Detroit Jazz Festival, there is something for everyone—and it is free!**

Overleaf: **Captain Dennis Neubacher in WJR's Traffic Copter circles over Hart Plaza and the celebrating crowds who line the riverfront, anxiously awaiting the International Freedom Festival fireworks display.**

"To me, Detroit is 'a work of art' that offers theatre, symphonies, entertainment, sports, Sindbad's, Greektown, Mexican Village, *and great people!*"

"Spike" Bell
Photographer
Windsor, Ontario, Canada

On rooftops along both sides of the riverfront, partygoers celebrate the International Freedom Festival. At Detroit's Omni, a combined apartment and hotel *(opposite)*, WJR's Joel Alexander and Dana Mills hosted one party, and on the 400 Tower mezzanine of Renaissance Center *(above)*, Coopers & Lybrand and Dykema Gossett hosted two other celebrations.

Overleaf: This spectacular view of the International Freedom Festival Fireworks against Detroit's beautiful skyline was taken by Windsor photographer, Spike Bell. We are grateful and honored to include both his warm sentiments about our city and his striking photograph in this book. It is most appropriate that our friend and neighbor, Canada, is represented in these pages.

The Hiram Walker Distillery, named for its founder, has a long history here with offices and roots in both Detroit and Windsor. Founded in 1858, it produces such well-known spirits as Canadian Club, Walker Special Old Canadian Whisky and Crystal Vodka. The beautiful Italian Renaissance structure which houses the administrative offices *(above)* celebrated its centennial this year.

"Detroit is a wonderful city. Many people are working diligently every day to make it a great place to live. My hometown is Louisville, Kentucky, but the Motor City is definitely my home away from home!"

Felecia D. Henderson
Editor, **On Detroit,**
The Detroit News

"Ask me about Detroit and I'll tell you about a city whose strength has always been its people; about a city whose vitality is reflected in the faces of a million people who came here from every corner of this nation, from every country on the globe, to give it life, to give it vigor, to give it hope in its own future. It's one of the reasons why I have always been proud to call it my home town."

Neal Shine
Publisher, The Detroit Free Press

Detroit is proud to have *two* Pulitzer prize-winning daily newspapers: the Detroit Free Press, founded May 5, 1831 by John Pitts Sheldon, and The Detroit News, founded August 23, 1873 by James E. Scripps. Many specially-focused publications also keep Detroiters informed, for example, business news magazines, ethnic newspapers and periodicals aimed at specific professional groups.

Overleaf: Located nearby is Riverfront Apartments, a popular residence for Detroit professionals who enjoy a spectacular view, private marina and tennis courts, and proximity to all the amenities that downtown Detroit offers.

"The 2,900 physicians and 16,000 employees of The Detroit Medical Center are proud members of the Detroit community. Not only do we want people to come here for their medical care, we want them to experience and learn for themselves all that Detroit has to offer. A wealth of medical, scientific and technological knowledge, the arts, our sports teams and our people make up some of the resources that can be found in Detroit. We are proud that several of our member hospitals have been a part of Detroit for more than 100 years and we are very excited about being part of this city's future."

David J. Campbell
President and CEO, The Detroit Medical Center

The lofty spires and Romanesque architecture of St. Josephat Catholic Church *(opposite)*, the fourth Polish church established in Detroit (1889), contrasts sharply with the modern structures of The Detroit Medical Center. Both, however, have a long history in the city. DMC's Children's Hospital of Michigan, Grace, Harper and Hutzel Hospitals, along with Wayne State University School of Medicine, have been in Detroit for more than a century. Including its more recent members as well—Detroit Receiving Hospital, Huron Valley Hospital, Rehabilitation Institute of Michigan, University Health Center and the several DMC Health Care Centers throughout the metropolitan area—The Detroit Medical Center is an integral part of the area's rich health care system.

Overleaf: Often referred to as the "City of Churches," Detroit's religious heritage can be found in its abundant houses of worship of all faiths. The strong ethnic roots of numerous parish communities reflect the rich and diverse history of this city. This view of Jefferson Presbyterian Church on the city's east side highlights its serene riverfront location.

"Detroit has a unique window of opportunity—the strength of its economy, the vision of its political leadership and the optimism of its people lead to the conclusion that exciting things will happen here."

Anthony F. Earley, Jr.
President and COO, Detroit Edison

"Detroit's skyline provides a glimpse of both our past greatness and our ongoing resurgence. These streets, which gave birth to the auto industry, will also be the path to our future greatness."

Frank E. Smith
President, Greater Detroit Chamber of Commerce

The varied architecture of Detroit's financial district *(opposite)* exemplifies much of the history of this city, from the ornate Guardian Building and stately Buhl and Penobscot Buildings to the modern NBD Bank and striking new One Detroit Center. A short distance away is Edison Plaza *(above)*, home of the city's electric utility company, Detroit Edison.
Referred to as the "Cathedral of Finance," the Guardian Building *(opposite, center)* was built by Smith Hinchman and Grylls Associates in 1929 as the Union Trust Building at a cost of $12 million. This magnificent example of art deco was designed by Michigan architect Wirt Rowland (who also designed the Penobscot Building) and is filled with unique pieces commissioned specifically for that building. In 1984, the Guardian Building became the corporate headquarters of MCN/MichCon, and they began restoring it to its original appearance.

"I love the University of Detroit Mercy. In the thirty-five years I taught there, I saw thousands of men and women graduate as professional architects, business leaders, teachers, lawyers, engineers, social workers, dentists and dental hygienists, and go on to serve the Detroit community as Michigan Supreme Court Judges, Mayors, school principals, heads of hospitals and scholars of national repute."

Arthur E. Loveley, S.J., Detroit

(Overleaf)

"We're very fortunate in Detroit to have several outstanding health care organizations that work together with the community's best interests as priority one. As one of those, Henry Ford Hospital has been committed to Detroit since it was founded in 1915 by Henry Ford. Over the years, Henry Ford Hospital has developed centers of excellence in heart and vascular disease, neurosciences, transplantation, bone and joint disorders, sleep disorders, genetics and birth defects and chemical dependency. We've grown into one of the nation's major comprehensive health systems, and we're very pleased to have done so in Detroit."

Gail L. Warden, President and CEO, Henry Ford Health System

DETROIT

The University of Detroit *(opposite)* **(founded in 1877) and Mercy College of Detroit (founded in 1941) consolidated in 1990 to form University of Detroit Mercy, Michigan's largest and most comprehensive Catholic university. With nine schools and colleges, it offers more than sixty academic fields of study. SS. Peter and Paul Jesuit Church, adjacent to the University of Detroit Mercy Law School *(above)* is one of the oldest churches in the city.**

Overleaf: **Henry Ford Hospital, located in the New Center, has been a leader in health care for generations in the Detroit metropolitan area.**

"Coming from New York, I was delighted to discover how friendly and generous the people are in this city. My husband and I arrived four weeks before our moving van, and our new neighbors, whom we had never met before, lent us furnishings and kitchen items to tide us over."

Barbara Goldman
Dykema Gossett, Detroit

"Often referred to as 'city of homes, trees and churches,' Detroit is also a birthplace of innovation. More importantly, Detroit is a place with the heart to make dreams come true."

Mary Ann McLaughlin
Dykema Gossett, Detroit

This neighborhood (*opposite*) near Cheyenne on the city's northwest side, is one of many lovely tree-lined residential communities in the metropolitan area. Detroit has long had an abundance of well-constructed single-family homes, ethnic neighborhoods and neighborhoods with historic designation. Recent resurgence in residential building has added brand new subdivisions, cluster housing and townhouses.

Overleaf: **An equally pleasant but very different kind of community can be found on Lake St. Clair Flats, northeast of Detroit.**

"Channel 7 is committed to making a difference in the community through outreach projects such as *Assignment: Education, Health-O-Rama, Brightest and Best, Immunization Fair* and *Operation Can-Do.* We often ask our viewers to support these and other programs and it's always heartening to witness the overwhelming generosity of the people in metropolitan Detroit."

Tom Griesdorn
General Manager
WXYZ-TV/Channel 7

WXYZ-TV/Channel 7, one of Detroit's four national network affiliates, signed on the air in October, 1948, from studios in Detroit. They moved into the newly constructed Broadcast House in Southfield *(left)* in May, 1959, a traditional Williamsburg Colonial style building with a 1,057-foot broadcast tower, which sits on a 110-acre tract of fields and streams.

EDS, with local offices in Southfield *(opposite)*, has operations in more than 30 countries, employs approximately 70,000 people worldwide and is the leader in applying information technology to meet the needs of businesses and governments around the globe.

Overleaf 1: This tranquil autumn scene near Wixom is typical of many rural areas that surround metro Detroit. Although all the other images in this book depict urban or suburban life, it would be incomplete without picturing the agricultural roots of this city.

Overleaf 2: Headquartered in an industrial park in Plymouth, Johnson Controls Automotive Systems Group is the world's largest supplier of automotive seating. In 1994, JCI produced seats for more than 6.5 million vehicles. The group employs more than 21,000 people at 90 facilities worldwide and had $2.55 billion in sales in 1993.

"Detroit is a city that is full of life and vitality. Chrysler Corporation has been a part of Detroit's history and we're proud to have many of our manufacturing facilities located here. We have grown together and contributed to making Detroit a great place to live and work. Our expectation for the future is continued growth and success."

Robert J. Eaton
Chairman and CEO, Chrysler Corporation

Chrysler Corporation, founded in 1925, produces Chrysler, Dodge, Eagle, Jeep and Plymouth cars and light trucks in 41 North American manufacturing facilities. In 1993, revenues totaled $43.6 billion, including vehicle sales of 2,476,000 cars, minivans, light trucks and sport utility vehicles sold by 7,000 dealers in more than 100 countries.

Chrysler Corporation's new 3.5 million-square-foot Technology Center in Auburn Hills *(above and opposite)* integrates the functions of product design, engineering, manufacturing, purchasing, finance and marketing. It also houses a pilot manufacturing plant, scientific test facilities and an evaluation road for testing vehicles in various stages of development.

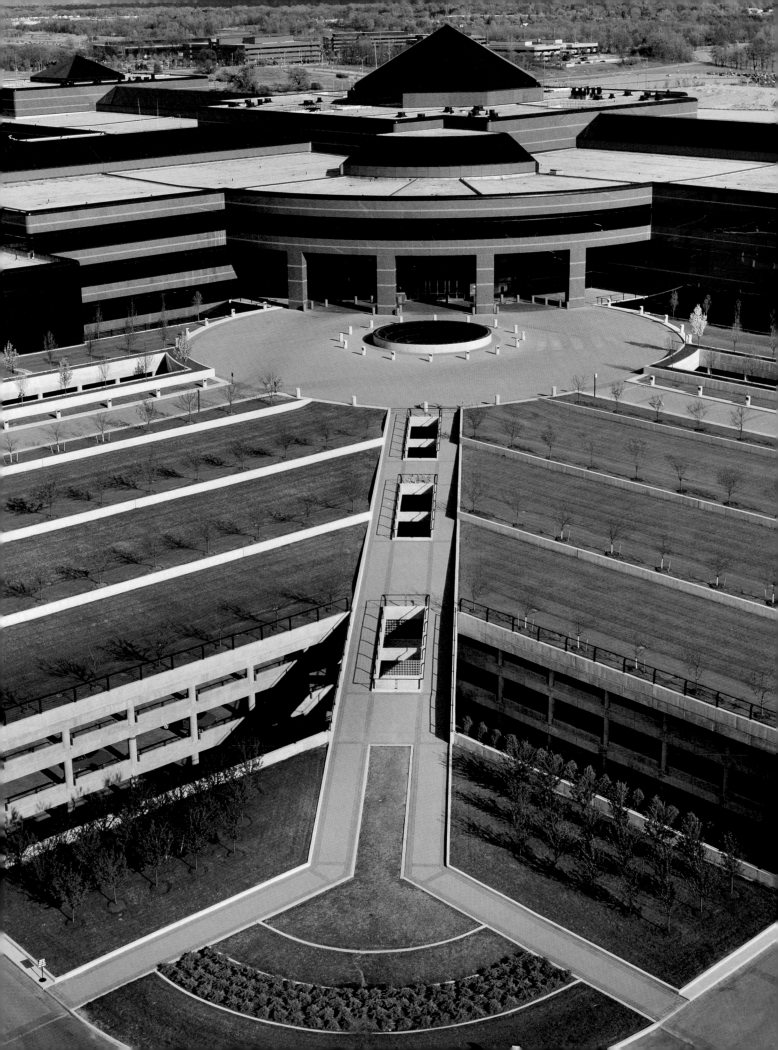

Meadow Brook Hall *(opposite)* was built in the 1920s by the widow of auto baron John Dodge. The grounds of this magnificent 100-room Tudor mansion in Rochester, now owned by Oakland University *(above, bottom)*, are the site of Meadow Brook Music Festival, a series of outdoor pop and classical concerts from June through September.

The entire area northeast of Detroit is rich with commerce, industry, fine restaurants and venues for sports and world-class entertainment. The Palace of Auburn Hills, home of the Detroit Pistons professional basketball team (winner of two consecutive NBA titles), and Pine Knob Music Theatre in Clarkston (both not shown) draw internationally-renowned performers to their stages. Troy, an important commercial center, is home to K-Mart World Headquarters *(above, top)*.

Overleaf: As we near the end of the journey, we return to where it began. The setting sun symbolically casts its warm glow on Detroit's skyline and an ocean-going vessel as it returns from delivering cargo to the Great Lakes.

"Zipping past Detroit monuments and skyscrapers and coasting through neighborhoods has become a ritual for our group of diverse and enthusiastic skaters. Besides invigorating both body and soul, these exhilarating city trips have become a wonderful social outing with some great economic side benefits, such as finding out about job and housing opportunities, patronizing dining and entertainment establishments, and for some, even meeting a future spouse."

Mary Hebert
Executive Director
Rivertown Business Association

(Overleaf)
"Working in the beautiful Fisher Theatre is a real bonus because it's in the elegant Fisher Building— a true art object to be treasured and revered."

Shirl Harris
Public/Community Relations Director
Fisher Theatre

This group of roller-bladers first began in 1989 with only five members. Within two years, after organizing an event called *Rolling on the River*, the group grew rapidly to about 300 and has stabilized around that level ever since. In addition to the wonderful exercise, the networking opportunities have resulted in 15 marriages! Other social/exercise groups, such as *Motor City Striders* and the popular and international *People Who Run Downtown*, get together regularly to walk, run or bicycle on Detroit's downtown streets.

Overleaf: The ornate Fisher Building, home to the beautiful 3,000-seat Fisher Theatre, also houses shops, a bank, restaurants and offices. Designed by Albert Kahn and completed in 1928, its illuminated "golden tower" and General Motors World Headquarters dominate the New Center skyline.

"Detroit is being reborn right before our eyes. One can feel the vibrancy as the rebirth of one of the greatest industrial cities in this nation begins. Detroit and Detroiters are winners...Always have been and always will be."

Robert N. Warfield
Executive V.P. and Treasurer, Alpha Capital Management, Inc.

Detroit's People Mover *(above and opposite)* is one of the most technologically advanced transportation systems in the world. A computerized control center, staffed by trained professionals, monitors the exact location and operating condition of each car at all times. The quiet, reliable, non-polluting Linear Induction Motors used on the People Mover vehicles utilize magnetic force for propulsion and braking — the first practical application of this technology in the United States. It takes only 14 minutes to travel the entire length of 2.94 miles of track, encircling the heart of downtown, which connects such attractions as Cobo Center *(opposite)* and Joe Louis Arena with Greektown and the Renaissance Center.

A special feature of the 13 conveniently-located stations (some of them actually *inside* downtown buildings) is the $2 million worth of art which has become one of Detroit's premier tourist attractions. *Art in the Stations,* an independent non-profit agency, commissioned regional, national and international artists to create a parade of images, moods, rhythms and colors that celebrate urban life and art and help to make People Mover travel an upbeat, enjoyable experience for the thousands who ride the system daily.

"Once or twice each year for many years now, on an evening when my wife was away, my three young daughters and I would take in the special atmosphere and flavor of Greektown. Octopus, flaming cheese, lamb chops and Gyros were followed by a stop at a pastry shop to pick up a late night snack to go. Each trip not only provided exposure to unique foods but, more importantly, created great memories of special times shared between a Dad and his girls."

Ken Castel
Dearborn Heights, MI

Greektown is one of Detroit's best-known and most loved nighttime entertainment districts. Monroe Avenue *(opposite)* is lined with a variety of ethnic restaurants, tavernas and bakeries—enough to tease any palate. Trapper's Alley, a multi-level marketplace in the historic tannery, offers a delightfully eclectic collection of specialty shops and restaurants. Visit the world's tallest indoor waterfall in The International Center atrium where 6,000 gallons of water rush over nine stories of Grecian marble every hour. Opened in 1992, The Atheneum *(above)* is a luxurious Suite Hotel and Conference Center housed in the converted former headquarters of the Ferry Seed Company. Several important historic churches can also be found in the Greektown area, including Old St. Mary's Catholic Church *(left)*, the Second Baptist Church and Annunciation Greek Orthodox Cathedral *(not shown)*.

Overleaf: "Detroit Aglow" had its beginnings in 1955 when the Central Business District Association became the catalyst for lighting up downtown Detroit for the holiday season. In 1985, CBDA sponsored the first Detroit Aglow Symphony Sing-Along to bring Detroiters and metropolitan neighbors and friends together to welcome the holidays with song. This much-loved annual November event kicks off the festive season encompassing Thanksgiving, Hanukkah, the Swedish Festival of Lights, Christmas and the New Year.

"Detroit, the largest city in Wayne County, is home to more scenes of beauty than most people would ever imagine. Nature put some of that beauty there: the riverfront, parks, and tree-lined neighborhoods. The rest? I think it must have come from Detroit's people. The hard work and effort of millions of people over three centuries have paid off—as hard work and effort always do—by turning many of the scenes of everyday Detroit into works of art."

Edward H. McNamara
Wayne County Executive

Our tour ends at the Renaissance Center, synonymous with Detroit and symbol of the City's rebirth since it opened in 1977. Six gleaming monumental round office/retail towers surround the 73-story Westin Hotel, one of the world's tallest. RenCen is practically a self-contained community with its many restaurants, a variety of specialty shops, and array of services such as dry cleaners, florist and post office. For entertainment, attend its theaters or explore The World of Ford product and technology display in Tower 300 which features a computerized system that allows visitors to "build" their dream car and assess its cost. The largest private development in the country when it opened, the Renaissance Center was the product of Henry Ford II's vision of a revitalized Detroit. He believed that it would serve as a catalyst for future growth—and that is exactly what it did.

Index